# THE

# DOIN

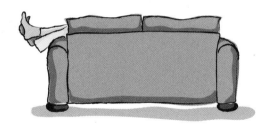

by
Jamien Bailey

**B3**

www.booksbyboxer.com

Published in the UK by
Books By Boxer, Leeds, LS13 4BS
© Books By Boxer 2015
All Rights Reserved

ISBN: 9781909732346

"To do nothing at all is the most difficult thing in the world; the most difficult and the most intellectual."

Oscar Wilde

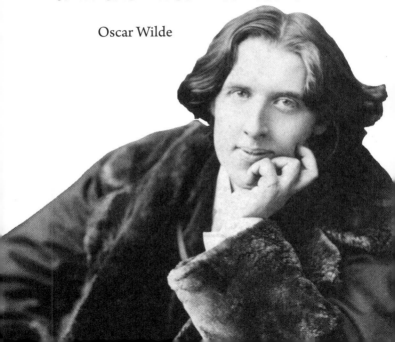

Doing nothing really is an art, a skill, a challenge and a feat of accomplishment.

If you can succeed in this difficult endeavour you should be jolly well pleased with yourself. So, find a nice comfortable spot, make yourself a cup of tea, put your feet up and start learning how less is the new more (more or less!).

Because of our ridiculous, fast-paced, hectic, stressful and work-obsessed lifestyles, doing nothing is considered to be either an idyllic dream or just plain idleness. But, for those dedicated individuals who are prepared to put a lot of hard work into perfecting the skill of doing nothing, there is an alternative way of looking at this pleasurable pastime!

Nothing comes without effort.

The act of doing nothing is derided as shirking, contemplating one's navel, fiddling while Rome burns: a negative and a waste of time. The implication is that you should be doing something more... useful. It takes a huge effort of will to overcome these ill-informed opinions.

So be bold, gentle reader, as you take to your chaise longue, your boudoir or bathtub. For these are the workplaces of the genius, the cradles of contemplation and philosophy: plus they're the places where you can skive off to for a couple of quiet hours.

Of course, laziness should not be at all encouraged (well, perhaps just a little, for the sake of this book) but life is not all about doing.

I would like to introduce a contrary theory, that doing nothing is essentially good: a necessity for your physical, mental and spiritual well-being. Doing nothing should be practiced by everyone on a regular basis; especially when you feel like you are being overworked!

# CHILDHOOD

"You are worried about him spending his early years doing nothing. What! Is it nothing to be happy? To skip, play, and run around all day long? Never in his life will he be so busy again."

Jean-Jacques Rousseau

Our inability to do nothing without guilt starts when we are young. For children, doing nothing is almost impossible. Children are good at doing what, to adults, seems like useless things: running, jumping and skipping; shouting, thinking and imagining; pretending, daydreaming and other such non-productive activities which, to a child, are the whole point of living.

"Time thinking and time dreaming is never time wasted."

Jonathan Swift

How many times were you told to stop daydreaming when you were a kid? At school, in the bad old days before teachers were told to stop picking on little 'uns, you would get the chalk thrown at you for daydreaming. Sometimes you deserved those chalky bruises but, at other times, the cogs of your nascent brain were turning more quickly than your ability to concentrate on your times tables.

As a kid, there was precious little time to daydream in the home. Whilst you were staring into space, contemplating the mysteries of the universe, your mother would throw the dish cloth at you, tell you to fetch some coal in, take the dog out or polish your shoes. And in those moments, that great spark of ingenuity, that E=MC2 stroke of genius that could have bubbled to fruition 20 years later, was lost: gone forever.

Einstein's mother, who was probably pretty smart herself, didn't have a dog or a dish cloth and probably had central heating, which is why Einstein was allowed more hours of daydreaming and turned out to be a genius.

# THE PLEASURE OF LEISURE

As we leave behind the cosy certainties of childhood, we find that time for leisure and relaxation disappears. These treasures now become rare luxuries to be savoured and cherished because, in the grown up world, there is always something to be done; something to finish and deadlines to be met. All of this comes with accompanying guilt, to be worn like a hair shirt and only removed upon completion of tasks.

# WORK IS WITH US: WORK IS EVERYWHERE

Work is here in all its exhausting and exhilarating forms: studying, careers, vocations; housework, gardening, DIY; fixing, cleaning, maintaining the car; looking after kids, keeping everybody happy and, sometimes, having to go out to work for a living.

Doing nothing now becomes a dream: an idyllic aspiration, a clarion call from a peaceful haven. Something that, if allowed, will distract you away from the washing up, the keyboard, the essential 'to-do' list, and all the other things that control our lives. This is precisely when you should stop and take some time out to do nothing for, according to

Hedon's Law, this is when your pleasure from leisure will be at its peak.

# HEDON'S LAW

"The Pleasure of Leisure (time) is directly proportionate to the number of hours worked prior to that leisure (time), multiplied by a factor of 2 in the case of unsatisfactory work and divided by a factor of 2 in the case of satisfactory work; i.e. the higher the number, the more Pleasure in the Leisure." OR, simply put: long hours of lousy work improve the quality of leisure time.

"Hard work never hurt anybody, but why take the chance?"

Anonymous

"The trouble with doing nothing is that you never know when you're finished."

Groucho Marx

# AVOIDING WORK

"Like the poor, pestilence and taxes, work will always be with us." (So wrote some lazy sod in the 18th century, whose name escapes me and I can't be bothered to look it up!)

Therefore, if there is no end to jobs to be done, it follows that leisure time must be found in the middle of work. An addendum to Hedon's law might be that the Pleasure of Leisure is enhanced by the amount of unfinished work and detritus that surrounds one.

"We're busy doing nothing, working the whole day through, trying to find lots of things not to do."

From the film, A Connecticut Yankee in King Arthur's Court

The maxim that work is never-ending has a particular relevance to work around the home and garden. This means you should plan your doing nothing time carefully. It's no use waiting until you finish a job, or finding a convenient stopping time because there will always be another job and never a convenient stopping time. It is absolutely essential that you stop right in the middle of the job, at the most inconvenient time possible. Wallow in the mess of paintbrushes, submerge yourself in the mass of papers on your desk, switch off when you're up to your knees in mud and tune out in the middle of the washing up. Take a break. Make a cup of tea. Read a book. Do nothing.

"Nirvana is not far away when you put your feet up on the desk."

James Pennington

Halfway through that complicated recipe you are preparing, stop; have a glass of wine.

When you have washed half the pots at the kitchen sink; walk away and have a lie down.

When you are in the middle of writing a book such as this switch off your computer and have a cup of tea.

As you sit in the midst of chaos and the debris of uncompleted tasks, contemplate your surroundings.

Delight in the unfinished business, the untidiness and the squalor that you have walked away from with gay abandon. Your doing nothing time will be enriched. Not only will you enjoy the deep satisfaction (if you are not used to doing it) of a naughty and rebellious act, you will continue your efforts with a renewed sense of vigour and optimism when (or if) you finally get back on the job.

"I am so busy doing nothing... that the idea of doing anything – which as you know, always leads to something – cuts into the nothing and then forces me to have to drop everything."

Jerry Seinfeld

# NEVER UNDERESTIMATE THE POWER OF UNDERACHIEVING

Not achieved your goal?
Not reached your target?
Missed your quota?
Not a team player?
Letting the side down?
Been snoozing and losing?

Erm... And your point is...?

Well, congratulations!

Instead of responding to jibes intended to motivate

the unmotivated, you have chosen to punctuate your busy schedule with some essential down time, a little bit of me time and still found the opportunity to sit down and do nothing. Now that is a real achiever!

Guilt? Don't even go there. Instead, repeat quietly to yourself "This is me, this is my time and this is what life is really all about. The tasks will be done later, OR THEY WON'T!"

However, I would agree that the world might not run quite as effectively (though, possibly, more peaceably) if everyone opted for the easier options. Therefore, choose moments when you will meet the least resistance. Some employers may not agree with the fine and proud declarations expressed here, so it may be wiser to restrict your rebellious inclinations to the home or garden.

"Do not underestimate the value of doing nothing"

Winnie the Pooh, A.A. Milne

# THE JOBS LIST

When you are given 'the list' (jobs given to you by your well-meaning, ever-loving, other half: the list of jobs that can't wait and must be done immediately), you must take charge of said list and reorganise it carefully. You must add do nothing after every three tasks (two, if you are feeling that way out)!

# PROCRASTINATION

"Never do today what can be put off until tomorrow"

Anonymous

You would not believe how long it has taken me to get round to writing this book! One of the problems of spending a supremely happy life in the pursuit of nothingness is that, when you need to do something particularly important (and to a timescale), it becomes all the more difficult.

"Work is a dividend paid to the future, for some imagined, but yet undefined, 'good' that will be bought from the proceeds of your present labour so that, when you look back to the past, you can consider it all worthwhile.'

Julien Goode

For society in general, procrastination is a very bad thing and the work ethic built into our souls from ancient times tells us that this is so. We are brought up with stuff like:

"The devil makes work for idle hands."

"If you don't work, you don't eat."

"Work is the curse of the idle classes."

... Or something like that!

And those who try their hand at doing nothing are

called, shirkers, malingerers, slackers, loafers, idlers and layabouts (amongst unprintable others). Doing Nothing is not for the fainthearted when there are others around. For a large section of society, it's akin to being caught with your fingers in the till or eating babies.

# THE ANCIENT ART OF DOING NOTHING

In the beginning, according to the bible, there was nothing... But later, there was also an awful lot of doing nothing.

Ancient man used to do very little but sit around all day in his cave, lighting the odd fire, doing nothing and waiting for the occasional mammoth to come along (usually one every three months, but sometimes two came along at once). Then, there would be a flurry of activity as ancient man and his buddies would catch, skin and chop up the mammoth, getting enough food, clothes and tools to last for three months, all in an afternoon. After that, it was doing nothing again for the next 3 months.

Ancient woman, although she would have you believe otherwise, didn't do an awful lot more (though she would look busy when other ancient women were around). There was little work to do in those caves; no point in cleaning. Cooking was throwing lumps of mammoth on the fire and there was no washing up to be done because they ate off flat pieces of wood and the 'pots' went straight on the fire. The weeks and months of interminable doing nothing would be punctuated only perhaps by a bit of seed crushing to make bread or porridge, or cooking a bit of mammoth on a hot stone every now and again.

This was the restful regime of the ancients. Hunting and gathering was more of a pastime, a hobby, a nice stroll out when the three walls (of the cave) became a bit unbearable. It's true that they probably only lived until about 22 but, crikey, did it seem longer, basking and malingering around in those long, blissful, lazy old prehistoric days.

How things have changed! We now can live to 92 but never seem to get a minute to sit down, cup in hand, to ruminate on our good fortune of longevity.

# BACK TO THE FUTURE

The Evolution of Efficiency:

"Do as much as possible today, to leave more time tomorrow, to do more things that can't be put off until the day after."

Anonymous

# REVISION

Learn by heart (or rote, whichever is the least exhausting) the following phrases:

WORK WILL ALWAYS BE WITH US.
DO NOT WAIT UNTIL THE WORK IS FINISHED TO TAKE A BREAK.
ALWAYS PUT OFF UNTIL TOMORROW THAT WHICH YOU CAN REASONABLY GET AWAY WITH TODAY.

# INTERNET

As Tim Berners-Lee, the inventor of the internet, famously didn't remark when his project was running late: www. (Work Will Wait)!

Note: the invention of the internet should have been ready by 1988 but wasn't completed until 1989 as the team kept going into 'sleep mode'.

"I don't understand people who like to work and talk about it like it was some goddamn duty. Doing nothing feels like floating on warm water to me. Delightful, perfect."

Ava Gardner

# THE SLOTH

"Sloths know how to live life in the slow lane. They have slow metabolism and a painfully slow digestive system which means that one third of their body weight, at most times, is the contents of their stomachs. Sloths travel at speeds of two metres a minute (.008 kilometres per hour) and often sleep 15 to 18 hours a day. For a mammal of their size (50-60 cm tall) they live a surprisingly long time, usually around 40 years if they avoid predators and poachers. It's a lifestyle not to be scoffed at."

Roger Parnes, wildlife expert

Inspiring! The sloth sits around all day, doing

nothing, and outlives most of his contemporaries, to a ripe old age of about 40. House flies and bees have a lifespan of about 4 weeks.

These winged creatures live incredibly short, but fabulously busy lives... go figure!

# SLOTH: THE SEVENTH DEADLY SIN

As one might expect from religion, SLOTH (laziness, apathy, doing nothing) is not considered a good thing.

"For Satan finds some mischief still for idle hands to do."

Isaac Watt, Against Idleness and Mischief

"When you get out of bed in the morning, feel your feet touch the ground and luxuriate in the feel of the carpet, your hand on soft clothes; smell the air from an open window and be ecstatic about the noises around you. Notice the colours around you and be thankful for these small gifts." Whoever wrote that didn't have to wake up with the alarm at

6.00am! But we appreciate the sentiment.

"Sitting quietly, doing nothing, spring comes and the grass grows by itself."

Zen proverb

# THE ART OF DOING THINGS SLOWLY

Things are generally done better if done more slowly; eating, drinking, making love; sharpening swords, diffusing bombs, negotiating with children; talking and breathing... especially breathing. Some ancient mystics consider life to be measured in the number of breaths we take. The optimum beneficial requirement seems to be 'take fewer but deeper breaths'. So, don't get too excited and don't rush about too much.

The slower you move, the more you will experience, so said the Ancient Monks of Kandahar, who weren't much into sports. Sometimes, if you really slow your senses down and concentrate, you can do almost impossible things, like pouring a glass of wine back in the bottle when you've had enough, without spilling more than half of it.

"It takes a lot of time to be a genius, you have to sit around so much doing nothing, really doing nothing."

Gertrude Stein

## THE SERIOUS STUFF
(yoga, meditation and relaxation techniques)

For those who just want a light read and do not want to be encumbered by 'health, well-being and mindfulness stuff' (what some might dismiss as superstitious mumbo jumbo claptrap), you can skip the next few pages and go have a lie down!

## HOW TO DO NOTHING WELL
(relaxation techniques)

Location is very important. You must be in safe, comfortable surroundings. You must not be disturbed. You need somewhere relaxing to sit or lie. You need peace and quiet. Switch off your mobile phone, take your landline off the hook; make sure computers, radios, TVs and music players are off and out of your space. Block out external noise by shutting the windows in your chosen space, if necessary (sounds of nature are acceptable). For some, casting off from these earthly comforts, the umbilical cords of the modern world, can be a disconcerting experience, but persevere.

Next, dim the lights a little. Loosen some of your clothing and sit still. You are going to do this for half an hour, an hour or whatever time you have allotted for the experience.

Sit or lie in your comfortable place. Tell yourself that this is what you want, it is going to help you cope better with life and that doing nothing is a good thing. Allow your thoughts to wander wherever your mind chooses. The only rule is that every thought must be positive or you will banish it and replace it by something nicer. You are not here to brood and ponder on problems, unless you can find a positive thought from this. If you have trouble in banishing negative thoughts, fill your mind with the following exercise:

Visualise number shapes starting with one, then two, then three, etc, taking time on each to establish a picture in your mind. This may be a house number style, an advert, a TV logo. Your imagination will find the images and, as you count in this way, your mind will randomly move on to something else. Providing it is a positive thought, allow it.

# HOW TO DO NOTHING WELL
(using meditation)

When you feel that your mind is stilled you can then try to meditate. This is not easy, but with a little time, it can be very beneficial. It is an attempt to control the senses and the mind which are generally free to wander, and this is achieved by giving your senses some small repetitive tasks which will allow your mind, body and spirit to balance in harmony with each other (expert tuition is recommended). The mind, body and spirit, the powerful forces that control your world, should be in perfect harmony, in equal balance.

Ideally sit cross-legged and fix your vision on some small point straight ahead (candle, design on wallpaper, point of light, etc, preferably not too bright). Touch your fingers together lightly, your forearms resting on your thighs. The senses of taste and smell generally do not need to be supressed.

For sound, a mantra is used. This is a simple word, often with no meaning, which is vocalised rhythmically in time with your breathing. The Buddhist mantra of "ohm" is used frequently but you can repeat, "mind, body, spirit" or any rich sound that can cut through the distractive thoughts in the brain.

# HOW TO DO NOTHING WELL
(basic yoga techniques)

True yoga is a mind and body work-out and is highly recommended as a means of achieving well-being, mindfulness and relaxation. It is available for all abilities, ages and levels of mobility.
Anyone who tries this under guidance of expert tuition will benefit.

Concentrating solely on the relaxation techniques and leaving aside the yoga positions for further study, the following is a small insight into this fascinating world. In keeping with the spirit of this book, yoga techniques should be learned slowly.

Apply all the aforementioned preliminaries of solitude and space and enter your chosen place with a respect for life attitude. This can be a difficult concept to embrace initially, but this engagement with the universe, the whole, the bigger picture of life, is really helpful in healing your soul.

This is purely a metaphor for getting the most out of doing nothing.

Loose or little clothing works best. You start by standing, legs slightly apart and hands loose. Eyes closed, drop your shoulders and breathe slowly. Breathe in by allowing the diaphragm (stomach area, below ribcage) to expand. At the end of the inhalation, pull in the diaphragm so that the lungs are inflated and just allow the air to drift away slowly.

After 4 or 5 breaths, sit on the floor and continue abdominal breathing, rhythmically, for a few more breaths. If you can, sit cross legged. Fix your stare straight ahead and continue breathing easily and slowly as you feel yourself relaxing. This is the point where you would continue with yoga exercises but for this book we will skip this part. Fix your gaze on a point in front of you and contemplate the task of bringing mind, body and spirit into harmony. When you feel you have achieved something from this, after 5 or 10 minutes, lay on your back with your eyes closed. You should not need any head support but you should be on a carpet, mat or rug.

Shake your limbs and wiggle a little to get into a comfortable, relaxing position. You are now going to relax your body step by step, starting from your feet and working gradually upwards. Wriggle your toes and move your feet saying, "I relax my feet, I relax my feet... they are relaxed" and then allow your feet to fall, relaxed.

Work your way up your body, back and front, following the above procedure for each, allowing each part to drop, relaxed, after repeating the phrase. When you reach the back of your head, move to the top, forehead, face and, finally, your eyes; breathing slowly and rhythmically throughout.

You should now be in a state of peaceful relaxation.

Now imagine yourself within your body, where nothing and no one can hurt you, like a baby in the womb. Fully at peace in this environment, being aware but not part of the outside world, you can now move mentally to a favourite (real or imagined) place, maybe a beach, side of a river, somewhere very peaceful. Enjoy the pleasure of this new environment of total relaxation. When practiced, it's quite possible to stay in this state for quite a long time without discomfort.

# THE AWAKENING

You decide when you want to emerge, but this should be done very slowly. Start by moving your fingers, limbs, body and raise yourself up. Stand and try to keep in this relaxed, aware state for as long as possible. Feel the carpet texture under your feet. Look with new eyes at everyday things. Use all your senses. Move slowly.

If this is done correctly and regularly, the benefits of well-being and mindfulness are tremendous and you can approach tasks with renewed vigour. You can deal with things that may have overwhelmed you before, things you thought too difficult to deal with.

# ZAZEN or ZEN

Zen meditation is a pure form, based on the teachings of Buddha.

Observing the breath is one of the techniques used to achieve total relaxation. The participant, seated in the lotus, half lotus or crossed leg position, often with a small cushion to sit on, observes and counts each breath, contemplating the life force. The observer impartially reflects on the awesome power of nature and the universe.

Observing the mind is another technique. The meditator contemplates his or her thoughts without engagement, allowing them to arise and pass away with no interference. This is the opposite of thinking. Worries are not actively shut out but observed and allowed to disappear one by one. Zoom out from your thoughts until they shrink into insignificance.

'Just Do It' could be a slogan for Zen, though the significance here is far less energetic and more contemplative than the sporting version of this phrase. The Zen idea is to just do one thing and not a multiple of things. If you are eating, just eat; if you are listening to music, just listen to music - don't try to read at the same time. Concentrating on only one thing de-clutters the mind. No room for multi-tasking here!

# GREAT ESCAPES

OK, that's enough of the serious stuff. How do you spend your time in the loo?

This next section covers escapes, bolt holes, sanctuaries and havens of peace, all within your easy distance. Hallowed places for those who just need to get away for a few minutes or a few hours or more without being disturbed.

# THE LOO

Even the busiest person has to go to the toilet
sometime so why not add 5 or 10 minutes of escape
time to do not a lot.

The loo is not just a convenient convenience, a place
where only perfunctory functions are performed and
for visits of need, it can also be a great place to
while away a short sojourn, a place where you have
a good reason to lock yourself away from others.
Although reading is not exactly doing nothing, it is
fairly close. Choose a light-hearted book with a few
frivolous facts, a book you can pick up and put down
easily... a book a bit like this one. Many books are

read in the wee place, in instalments. Languages are learnt, great ideas are generated, speeches are written and plans are made in this small but cosy bolt hole.

Do not underestimate the amount of newsprint, crap books, comics and serious tomes that can be digested and the amount of irrelevant knowledge that can be accumulated by 5 or 10 minutes reading per day in this studio. It is rumoured that Shakespeare was an avid reader on his olde commode and he wrote there quite a bit as well. He may have been inspired in the midst of his ablutions to write the immortal lines... "Don't waste thy time in windy argument but let the matter drop" from Julius Caesar.

If you are happy with the atmosphere of the loo,
this is the place to hang out.

# THE GARDEN

The requirements for garden escapes are usually good weather conditions and this makes an ideal summer retreat to indulge you in a dollop of nothingness. It is easy to look busy in a garden, looking purposefully at plants, taking a rest under the trees, loitering in the greenhouse, lurking in the lupins, whilst actually doing nothing.

# SHEDDING YOUR INHIBITIONS

Sheds were created specifically for people (mostly men but quite a few women) as a place for escape.

Sheds, places where undefined projects are taking place and mysterious objects are concealed are the last vestiges of refuge left to urban dwellers. The word pottering (OED definition, occupy oneself in a desultory but pleasant way) originated in the shed.

Make sure your shed is wind and rainproof, has a comfortable seat, lots of books and magazines and preferably a kettle. Leave your phone and other 21st century gadgets in the house. This is a perfect bolt hole. You could be in there for long periods before they come and find you.

DO NOT DISTURB

# THE BEDROOM

A very comfortable place to hide, if a bit obvious. If done sneakily, you might get away with it for half an hour. The best way to 'do nothing' in the bedroom is to lie down and have a short nap. When they find you are missing they will be onto you pretty quickly.

# THE BATHROOM

Now we're talking! Another great excuse to lock yourself away for an hour or two. A bath is taking doing nothing to a higher level. It's the ultimate place to be doing nothing. Ensconced in your suds it's difficult to imagine any thought of doing something.

Great thoughts can come to you in the tub and you may have a "Eureka" moment (said by Archimedes when he realised that the dirty water displaced by his body could be used to measure volumes of odd shaped objects). "You reek a bit" was actually what his wife said before he got into his twice yearly bath!

Some like to read, eat, drink tea, send emails, watch TV, do their weekly washing or sleep in the bath; all fraught with potential dangers. There are too many activities going on with these activities so it's best just to do nothing at all.

# OUTDOOR ESCAPES

Not everyone's ideal place to unwind but a leisurely drive in the country can prove very relaxing.
Turn off the radio and concentrate purely on driving at a steady speed, preferably in good weather. Pull over somewhere quiet and have a sleep before a leisurely drive home.

A walk in the woods or the park can also provide the opportunity for a snooze in warm weather. Make sure you are far enough away from kids, dogs, hawkers, stalkers and pickpockets

# RETAIL THERAPY

This can be relaxing, though many men would disagree. Avoid crowded areas and enjoy all the experiences, including queuing.

Queuing, standing in line, is generally a bad experience leaving you frazzled and frustrated, annoyed at time being wasted. Use queuing as a positive activity, an observation point to study your fellow human beings and their habits. Beware.
Some habits of your fellow human beings can be pretty disgusting.

"When was the last time you spent a quiet

moment just doing nothing — just sitting looking at the sea or watching the wind blowing the tree limbs, or waves rippling on a pond, a flickering candle or children playing in the park?"

Ralph Marston

# THE CAFE

A favourite cafe is one of the best places to do nothing. Many hours can be idly and pleasantly passed in a people watching seat, where good coffee and tea are dispensed in comfortable surroundings.

You can just do nothing or browse your book or magazine in blissful repose in the aroma-filled atmosphere of a caffeine haven, lulled by the gentle murmurs of conversation, the bustle of the baristas and the gurgling, bubbling, boiling and steaming of the Gaggia, behind the counter. They are the sounds and smells to settle the soul on a frosty mid-morning or a sunny afternoon.

# WATCH THE EXPERTS

Animals are experts at doing nothing. Cats and dogs just love to laze around and can stay in almost the same place and the same position – seemingly for hours – whilst their human counterparts are running all around them, being busy.

Humans tolerate this inactivity but secretly resent it. The general feeling of the harassed owner is, "Why should I run around cleaning the house, getting the food, shopping for your stuff, working all hours, and the rest, and all you do is slob around all day finding it an effort even to scratch your butt or sniff your crotch?"

We have to be more like them. Your cat or dog would tell you to reduce your dependence on things that require work, like a clean house, cooked food, washing and ironing, keeping yourself clean and tidy, repairing things, making appointments, on the phone, on the computer and, of course, going out to work. All of these are things that an animal considers unnecessary and wonders why the heck you don't just sit still.

Obviously, this is not practical for most people, though some seem to do rather well on it. However, curling up on the rug in front of the fire and having a good scratch and a sniff under one's armpits is a must try before being discounted.

"Dogs are our link to paradise. They don't know evil or jealousy or discontent. To sit with a dog on a hillside on a glorious afternoon is to be back in Eden, where doing nothing was not boring — it was peace."

Milan Kundera

"If there really was a fair god your dog would trot straight into heaven while you would still be outside the gates, negotiating"

Mark Twain

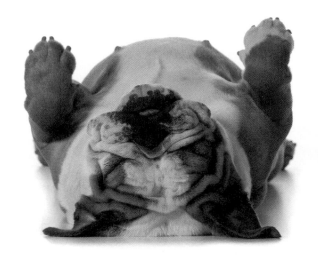

# DO NOTHING AT WORK AND STILL GET PAID

There is a real skill to doing this and a few essential rules to follow to ensure your survival. Only in certain types of employment can you get away with this and the office is a natural place to become an exponent of the art. Ideally, being slightly higher than the dogsbody on the bottom rung of the ladder is a better place to be for doing nothing (in other types of employment you wouldn't get away with it quite so easily, a bricklayer's mate for instance).

In the office you will need to follow a few tried and tested techniques:

- Look busy! Make your desk resemble ordered chaos; full in-tray, papers in little piles, half written notes, Post-it notes everywhere, your phone constantly ringing (even if it's you dialling in from your mobile)!
- Walk around briskly with papers or files under your arm looking a bit stressed.
- No time to stop for lunch. Ask a colleague to bring you something back. Eat while you are hitting the keyboard and shuffling papers.
- Speak quickly so work colleagues think you are too busy even to speak to them.
- Position your computer screen so it can't be seen

easily.

- Use 'work friendly', when you are watching all the non-work stuff on the internet. This website will turn a game or some unsuitable content on the screen into a boring looking word document in a split second at the touch of a key if someone gets too near.

- Time off. Start planning in advance, allowing your 'symptoms' (coughs, temperatures, ageing relative at death's door, etc.) to develop in the office. Pick illnesses that are hard to quantify such as migraines, allergies, lower back pain, 'some sort of virus' or irritable bowel syndrome, things that colleagues won't want to discuss or don't want to catch. Use you acting skills when phoning in, "he/she sounded so awful on the phone", is the office equivalent of an Oscar.

- Sick kids. This is always a winner and if you don't have kids there are always dependent relatives, your sister's kids or ageing pets that need urgent attention.

- Make a note of your lies. Research your illnesses and don't overdo it.

- Find hiding places. The stock cupboard, the spare office that's never used, the car park and even the loo as a last resort.

- Have a good excuse in advance why you can't work late.

- Never volunteer for anything.

- Never learn new skills and if you do have brilliant

skills, keep them to yourself.

- Lie about how long things take. If you declare that something will take 4 hours, you do it in 1 hour, announce that you have completed the task after 2 hours, then you will look good even though you skived for a good hour at least.
- Set up systems that only you know that makes a job look like it is taking hours when it can be done in minutes.
- Come up with ideas, however ridiculous, to show you are conscientious and thinking about the company but don't volunteer to carry them out. Nominate someone who is, 'much more skillful at this kind of thing'.
- Finally, find a job where there are long periods

of doing nothing, like night security, house sitting, or most jobs in middle management. Or find a job where there are long periods of doing nothing interspersed with short periods of frenetic and possibly dangerous activity such as; long distance air crew, firefighters or senior police officers.

# TAKE A LONG FLIGHT

For the devoted 'doing nothinger', this is as good as it gets: sitting down in a comfortable armchair surrounded by gadgets. Food and booze delivered to your armchair at regular intervals. Being unreachable and incommunicado for the duration of the flight and literally in a world of your own as you blissfully float through the clouds, anticipating the excitements to come at journey's end.

Europe to the Far East is usually around 12 or 13 hours, just enough time to eat, drink, watch films, play games, read, dream and sleep, completely undisturbed by the demands of the world on terra firma.

The longest scheduled flights (2015) are:

- Jeddah to Los Angeles
  17 hours, 20 minutes (at certain times of the year)
- Dallas to Hong Kong
  17 hours, 5 minutes (at certain times of the year)
- Dallas, to Sydney
  16 hours, 55 minutes
- Johannesburg to Atlanta
  16 hours, 40 minutes
- Abu Dhabi to Los Angeles
  16 hours, 25 minutes
- Dubai to Houston
  16 hours, 35 minutes

The flight from Newark (N.Y.) to Singapore was,

until 2013, the longest scheduled flight. This service was discontinued in November of that year due to low profitability. Aboard this Singapore Airlines Airbus A340 flight, a person could have been doing nothing for just short of 19 hours (18 hours and 50 minutes is the official time).

Perhaps the ultimate long flight experience will be the one way trip to Mars and you'll need a good book for that one.

# EXTREME WAYS OF DOING NOTHING

Yogis, the holy men of the Indian sub-continent, are able to bury themselves underground for long periods by slowing down their breathing and their metabolism and meditating fiercely. There are others who can spend a cold night sitting outside on a snow covered hillside, half naked, and feel no ill effects. To this day there are possibly thousands of yogis meditating in caves in the Himalayas in extreme conditions. Well, good luck to them, but there are easier ways to achieve a similar experience.

# ISOLATION TANK

The isolation tank, also known as a sensory deprivation chamber or flotation tank, was first devised and used by John C. Lilly a medical practitioner and neurophysicist. His early experiments, often involving the use of LSD, were made to try to find out what the brain does when fully deprived of sensory stimulation. Nowadays, the isolation tank is used as a well-being and mindfulness alternative therapy tool to promote relaxation, meditation and self-healing.

Practitioners swear by the benefits of floating around, doing nothing, which, they say, improves creativity, super learning, relief from stress and hundreds of other health benefits. The tank is completely dark and without sound or smell. At the bottom is a shallow depth of salt water heated to skin temperature in which the participants float naked, usually in the supine (laid on the back) position though pregnant women are recommended to use the opposite, prone position, chin on forearms. Apparently, this is a joyful experience and one can lay for hours, generally without the need for re-positioning, unlike in bed when blood flow can be restricted and force you lie in a different way. Probably not for the claustrophobic, but a whole new industry has sprung up around this therapy, particularly in California, as one might expect. For

fairly close to perfection, a place to hide and idle away the hours suspended in a plastic 'womb' with all the justifications of health and wellness with a touch of creativity thrown in. Heavenly!

# MOVERS AND SHIRKERS

It would seem that some great people of the past also like to indulge in a little, doing nothing and this is probably their secret to success. Archimedes, who we have already discussed, was lazing around in his bath when he made one of his most important discoveries. Isaac Newton was dozing underneath a tree when an apple fell on his head and he discovered gravity. Well, gravity was already discovered but Isaac created a simple theory that we could all understand:

$$Fg = G\ m1m2r2$$

Every particle of matter in the universe attracts

every other particle with a force that is directly proportional to the product of the masses of the particles and inversely proportional to the square of the distance between them. It's as simple as that!

Einstein warns us against too much activity and really he is saying "do nothing and great things will happen."

"Reading, after a certain age, diverts the mind too much from its creative pursuits. Any man who reads too much, and uses his own brain too little, falls into lazy habits of thinking."

Albert Einstein

Nero, instead of running around shouting, grabbing

buckets of water in each hand and yelling at the inadequacies of the Roman fire services, decided to get his fiddle out and play a few jiggy tunes, or the Italian equivalent, whilst Rome was burning to the ground.

Jesus was no shirker; however, he did decide to disappear into the desert for 40 days and 40 nights.

Jonah, in the Biblical story, took refuge inside a whale to get away from it all for a few days.

Louis the 14th (The 'Sun' King/Louis Quatorze) was in some ways quite a lazy monarch, having special ceremonies in the mornings and evenings, the 'levees' and the 'couchees' where his attendants and most of the court would vie for the right to do the most small and intimate service so that the king could immerse himself in the absolute joy of doing nothing.

In spite of this apparent indulgence, France was at the height of its greatness during his reign.

Otis Redding, who had a prolific creative output in his short life, also hankered for quiet contemplation with a little bit of doing nothing on the side. His iconic record, 'Dock of the Bay', (watching the ships roll in, and I watch them roll away again) is the idle dreamers anthem of a perfect day doing nothing. Shortly after writing the song, Otis sadly died in a plane crash, and the record became the first posthumous number one in the US charts.

Even the British football Premier League has its place in the Movers and Shirkers section. There can be few players who have not been accused by their frustrated fans of 'doing nothing' for most of the game.

# OPPORTUNITIES TO DO NOTHING

Now that humans have become conditioned to constant work, we need excuses to be able to do nothing. Being stuck in a lift, stuck in traffic, waiting for a delayed flight, a train cancelled, stuck at home with measles, these are all opportunities to switch off, however, it's pretty impossible to enjoy the joys of doing nothing in a four mile traffic jam.

On the contrary, to be snow-bound and stranded in a cosy inn with fun people, or sitting on a train opposite an attractive stranger would make doing nothing for a few hours a completely different —and possibly life-changing — experience.

However, there is one joyous time when you can do nothing in the most delightful of circumstances and that is at Christmas (after the hectic run up to the event that is). This is one of the few times that you can get away with it, so make the most of this festive feast of fun.

Once the dinner has been served, the pots have been dealt with and everyone is merry and bright, you can indulge yourself – without guilt – in the absolute joy of doing nothing, or next to nothing, if you are to include the occasional scoffing of sweets, treats and chocolates, drinking the odd glass or two, and discovering the joys of Christmas TV.

This can – and should – last for days as you contemplate the leisurely holiday you will take next year, lazing in the sun, doing the same sort of nothing as you are doing now. For a few precious days you can forget the exercise that you have vowed to do in the New Year in order to look gorgeous for your dream holiday. Not to mention the hard work you will have to do in order to pay for it!

# THERAPEUTIC BENEFITS

In conclusion, doing nothing isn't really doing nothing but, in most cases, doing nothing useful.

Sometimes being busy is an excuse to cover thoughts that would otherwise inconveniently come to the surface. It is through doing nothing that we are able to confront, contemplate and finally come to terms with things that trouble us. It allows us to formulate positive plans for future happiness and well-being. Just like a computer, the brain responds positively to down time, to renew and refresh brain cells and patterns and to process data. It is during rest that most acquired facts and knowledge are consolidated in the brain. The refreshed brain is able to task better, perform more logically and with renewed vigour.

It is easier to respond to the calls from the business world, to look at your computer, phone or tablet; to pick up a newspaper or magazine; to switch on the TV or radio than it is to fixate your thoughts into the practice of doing nothing for a short time.

This is why doing nothing is not as simple to do as one imagines and the disciplines shown in this book will help you to achieve the joy that is possible from this inactivity.

# THE ABSOLUTE JOY OF DOING NOTHING

At the end of the day, or more precisely, at the start of the day, one of the easiest and most satisfying ways of taking extra time doing nothing is to have a lie in in the morning. A few hours of blissful dozing, lying and ligging in your comfortable bed whilst the weather is howling and the world is rushing by outside, is an immeasurable pleasure that must be seized (quite the opposite thought of Horace, in his book of Odes in 23 BC. Carpe Diem... Seize the Day).

So, in conclusion, enjoy your relaxation and leisure; your escapes and snoozes; the pleasure of doing things slowly and stopping in the midst of work, without fear of guilt or recrimination. Remember that periods of doing nothing are good for you, will make you more efficient, less grumpy and more healthy.

"You have to allow a certain amount of time in which you are doing nothing in order to have things occur to you, to let your mind think"     Mortimer Adler

Learning to appreciate the absolute joy of doing nothing is a life changing experience and brings benefits to those who embrace this slower lane of life. Therefore, start right away. Find a nice soft couch to lie on, put your feet up and find the absolute joy of doing nothing.

Now go forth...

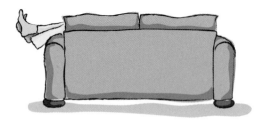

and do absolutely nothing!